DEVOTION TO ST JUDE

by
Glynn MacNiven-Johnston

*All booklets are published thanks to the
generous support of the members of the
Catholic Truth Society*

CATHOLIC TRUTH SOCIETY
PUBLISHERS TO THE HOLY SEE

ISBN 978 1 86082 395 4

Contents

WHO WAS ST JUDE?

What we know about St Jude

We can be certain about very little concerning St Jude's life on earth. Even his name is wrong: he, like Judas Iscariot, was called Judah.

We do know that he was one of Christ's disciples. Two of the twelve were called Judah (in Greek, Judas) and so they had to have other names to distinguish them from each other. One was called Iscariot because of where he came from (Kerioth), and the other was called Thaddeus or Lebbaeus, which could mean that he had a burly chest or that he was big-hearted. It was only later, when the name Judas had the connotations of betrayal, that Judas Thaddeus became Jude.

From the Gospels we know very little about St Jude. He is named as one of the Twelve, as Jude in *Luke* and *John* and as Thaddeus in *Matthew* and *Mark*. *Luke* and the *Acts of the Apostles* refer to him as 'James's Jude', perhaps referring to James the Less, who may have been his brother - but that too is unsure since James (Jacob) was a common name. Normally we would assume that the James referred to was Jude's father, and some translations use that form, but it was not uncommon for people to be named in reference to another relative who was well-known. In the lists of the Apostles he comes immediately after 'James son of Alphaeus', which some have seen as linking him to that James.

Jude may have been one of the 'brothers' of the Lord (James, Joseph, Simon and Jude) mentioned in *Matthew* 13:55 and *Mark* 6:3, where people who have grown up with Jesus wonder how he can be speaking with so much authority. If he is that Jude, it would make him a close relative of Jesus's (the Aramaic word *aha* is used to describe brothers, cousins and other relatives); but that may have been a different Jude altogether.

Jude is only recorded as speaking once, in *John* 14:22. At the Last Supper, Jesus is trying to prepare his disciples for what will happen next. Jesus says, 'in a little while the world will see me no more but you will see me...' The Jews believed that when the Messiah came, the whole world would see him, which is why Jude asks, 'Lord, how is it that you will manifest yourself to us and not to the world?' People have inferred lots of things about Jude's character from this, but most importantly it shows us is that he knew Jesus to be the Messiah and he believed Jesus could answer his question. The only other appearance of Jude is at Pentecost. According to the *Acts*, all the disciples were present at Pentecost, and statues of St Jude usually show him with a flame above his head to indicate this.

Jude's letter

The New Testament also contains the *Letter of St Jude* which, from early times, tradition has ascribed to the Apostle Jude. Again, there are those who believe from the style and vocabulary that it is a later work, but other scholars say that if it were later it would contain reference to the destruction of Jerusalem (AD 70). The early theologians Origen and Tertullian believed it was Jude the Apostle's own letter, as did Clement of Alexandria, who wrote a commentary on it.

The author of the letter introduces himself as a 'servant of Jesus Christ and brother of James'. From *Acts* and the *Letter of St Paul to the Galatians* we know that James, the brother (i.e., close relative) of the Lord, was one of the leaders of the church in Jerusalem and therefore well-known and respected by the Christian communities. We do not know who this letter was sent to (it could apply to all Christians), but it may have been sent to the same people that the *Letter of James* was sent to. It is also probable that they were Jewish Christians since Jude alludes to Jewish traditional stories from the *Book of Enoch* (verses 14-15) and the *Assumption of*

Moses (verse 9). The purpose of the letter is to call the community back to faith in its fullness, to live a moral life and not to follow the false teachers who had infiltrated their community.

Traditional stories about St Jude

Tradition has quite a lot to say about St Jude. *The Golden Legend*, a medieval collection of lives of the saints by Jacobus de Voragine, says that Simon, James the Less and Jude were all brothers, the sons of Alphaeus and Mary of Cleophas (see *Luke* 19:25). The Eastern Orthodox tradition even gives Jude's wife's name, Maryam (another form of Mary). Eusebius, an early historian, speaks of Jude's grandsons, James and Zoker. He quotes St Hegesippus, a 2nd century writer, who says that the Emperor Domitian had ordered the execution of all the descendents of King David because he was afraid they would claim his throne.

'And there still survived of the Lord's family the grandsons of Jude... These were informed against by some heretics as being of David's line and brought...before Domitian Caesar, who was as afraid of the advent of Christ as Herod had been. (*Matthew* 3-4) Domitian asked them if they were descended from David and they admitted it. Then he asked them what property they owned and what funds they had at their disposal. They replied that they had only 9,000 denarii between them...[which was] not available in cash but was the estimated value of the twenty-five acres of land, from which they raised the money to pay their taxes and the wherewithal to support themselves by their own toil.' Then, Hegesippus says, they showed the emperor 'as proof of their toil, the hardness of their bodies and the calluses impressed on their hands by incessant labour.' Domitian then asked about Christ and his Kingdom and 'they explained that it was not of this world or anywhere on earth but angelic and in heaven and would be established at the end of the world when Christ would come in glory to judge the living and the dead and give every man payment according to his conduct. On hearing this Domitian found no fault with them, but despising them as beneath his notice, let them go free and issued orders terminating the persecution of the church in Jerusalem.'

Jude and Agbar

One of the most well-known stories about St Jude begins in Edessa, the capital of a small kingdom in the area of what is now Urfa in southern Turkey. The king of Edessa, Agbar V 'The Black', had contracted leprosy and, having heard of Jesus's miracles, wrote to ask Jesus to come and heal him. Eusebius quotes the letter as well as Jesus's alleged reply:

Agbar's letter sent via his messenger, Ananias:

'Agbar, Ruler of the city of Edessa, to Jesus the Saviour, the good physician, who has appeared in Jerusalem, Greetings -

I have heard about you and about the cures you perform without medicine or herbs. What I have heard is that you make the blind see again and the lame walk, you cleanse lepers, expel unclean spirits and demons, cure those who have suffered from chronic and painful diseases, and raise the dead. On hearing all this about you, I concluded that one of two things must be true - either you are God and came down from heaven to do these things, or you are God's son doing them. I am therefore writing to ask you to come to me and cure the illness from which I suffer. I have heard that the Jews are treating you badly and wish to cause you harm - my city is very small, but very noble, adequate for both of us to live in peace.'

Jesus's reply:

'Blessed is he who has never seen me and yet believes in me. Long ago it was written that those who see me will not believe in me and that those who have not seen me will believe in me and be saved. As to your request that I visit you, it is better

for me to stay here and finish the work I was sent to
do. After I have finished, then I will be taken up to
him who sent me. Then I will send you one of my
disciples to heal your disease and bring salvation to
you and your people.'

Eusebius says he read these letters in a Greek
translation of the original Aramaic and did not question
their authenticity. These days they are dismissed as
forgeries, although some people believe these were
spoken messages which were written down later. In any
case, the letters were cherished relics in Edessa and
were widely believed to protect the city - so much so
that, when the Persians besieged the city, Christ's letter
was held aloft on the city walls and the Persians were
defeated. The letters, forgeries or not, have disappeared
in the mists of time but are rumoured to be held in a
monastery in Kyrgyzstan.

Portrait of Jesus

King Agbar had also commissioned a portrait of Jesus,
but the painter was unable to paint him. Jesus, feeling
sorry for the man, pressed a cloth to his face and an
image miraculously appeared. This was called the
mandylion (a small cloth or handkerchief). One
tradition says that this cloth was delivered to Agbar by

St Jude, and this is one explanation of the large portrait medallion of Jesus that statues of St Jude are shown wearing. The cloth was venerated in Edessa and then, after AD 945, in Constantinople, in the Hagia Sophia (Church of the Holy Wisdom). During the Fourth Crusade in 1204, the cloth disappeared. There are many claims as to what happened to it next. It could be the cloth in the church of San Bartolomeo degli Armeni in Genoa. It has also been linked to the Sudarium, another cloth kept in Oviedo Cathedral.

Preaching and martyrdom

Various sources say that when the disciples went out to the world, Jude went first to Edessa to fulfil Jesus's promise to Agbar. Eusebius says Jude stayed there in the Jewish quarter with a man called Tobias. According to *The Golden Legend*, Jude cured Agbar by wiping his face with Christ's letter and Agbar was converted, as were many other people in Edessa. Jude stayed in Edessa for five years building up the community before moving on to Armenia. The Armenian church identifies St Jude with their St Addai, and the liturgy of Addai and Mari is still in use today in the Eastern Rite. Jude then brought the gospel to Mesopotamia (modern Iraq) and Pontus (the Black Sea coast of Turkey) before he met up with Simon, another of the Twelve and possibly

Jude's brother, in Persia (modern Iran), where they began to evangelise together.

In Persia, again according to *The Golden Legend*, Simon and Jude had to defeat two sorcerers called Zaroes and Arphaxat, who had been driven out of Egypt by Matthew. There is a story that the two Apostles and the sorcerers were asked to predict the outcome of an impending battle. When the Apostles predicted correctly, the crowd turned against Zaroes and Arphaxat, who were only saved when Jude and Simon pleaded for them to be spared. Far from being grateful, however, the sorcerers continued their persecution of Jude and Simon and, at Suanir, when the Apostles refused to sacrifice to the gods, the sorcerers incited a mob and Jude and Simon were martyred. Jude was clubbed into unconsciousness, then had his head cut off with an axe, which is why he is sometimes represented with a club and sometimes with an axe. Simon was sawn into bits. Suanir is identified by some with Colchis on the Black Sea coast of the Republic of Georgia. (Curiously, Colchis is well known in Greek legend as the shrine of the Golden Fleece.)

Jude and Simon were the only two Apostles to be martyred together. Their bones rest under the altar of St Joseph in St Peter's Basilica in Rome, marked by a small, barely visible plaque; in 1548, Pope Paul III granted a plenary indulgence to anyone who visits their tomb on their joint feast day, 28th October.

There are other legendary tales about St Jude which seem highly implausible to modern readers, but this should not blind us to the reality of St Jude's mission on earth, or to the real conviction people have had of St Jude's power as an intercessor. Many later saints have had a devotion to Jude, including St Bernard of Clairvaux, who carried a relic of St Jude and was buried with it.

St Jude, Patron of things despaired of

Perhaps the stories are embroidered, perhaps we know very little about his life on earth, but we can be sure that many people have received help through his intercession.

Legend has it that St Jude was distressed no one prayed to him because, since he shared a name with Judas Iscariot, people thought their prayers would be 'delivered' to the wrong Judas, to the one who could not help them! So St Jude, this version of the story says, promised to intercede for all those whose situation was hopeless, impossible. He became the saint of last resort. However only Jude amongst the Twelve has such a devoted following. The others are revered, admired, and even imitated, but do not have St Jude's astonishing reputation as an intercessor. Perhaps it is more likely that he became the saint of the despairing and desperate because the *Letter of St Jude* speaks of reassuring the doubtful and pulling out those who need to be saved from the fire (*Jude* 22-23). Whatever the reason, God seems to have allowed St Jude the power to help even where others have failed.

Christians have always asked others to pray for them, to intercede with the Father, and praying to a saint is no different from asking this of a friend or a priest. When people ask the intercession of a saint, they often like to have a place to focus on and shrines 'happen'. Sometimes these are places associated with the saint during his or her lifetime, but sometimes they have grown up independent of any physical association.

National Shrine of St Jude, Faversham

There are many shrines to St Jude throughout the world but, although we can see from *The Golden Legend* and other similar works that there has been devotion to St Jude from early times, most of the shrines are fairly modern. This is possibly because places associated with St Jude during his lifetime are in countries no longer Christian. In Britain, of course, because of the history of the Catholic church here, most shrines have been set up in the last hundred years.

The Shrine of St Jude in Faversham, Kent -
including a reliquary, a copy of a silver monstrance of
1547, containing a fragment of bone from St Jude -
was dedicated on 28th October 1955 in an annex of
the parish church of Our Lady of Mount Carmel. The
shrine came into being in quite a strange way. In the
1930s the Carmelite friars had a small press there,
printing amongst other things religious pictures which
they sold to help support themselves since they were
only recently re-established in England. Concentrating
on representations of Our Lord and Our Lady, they did
not initially print images of St Jude, but many people
nevertheless wrote asking for pictures of him. As Fr
Elias Lynch, O. Carm., who was in charge of
Faversham, recalled: 'In the end, we decided that the
only way out was to print a large number of pictures
of St Jude and send them out to everybody. I found an
old German picture of St Jude with a club big enough
to murder anyone, and I reproduced a quarter of a
million pictures of St Jude and his club, with prayers
in honour of St Jude, and sent them out...I got more
than a surprise. I was caught in a tidal wave. People
started sending in Masses of thanksgiving to St Jude;
donations to the Shrine of St Jude - which didn't exist;
petitions to the Shrine of St Jude - which didn't
exist... The upshot of it was that we decided to create

a Shrine of St Jude, Apostle and Martyr, Patron of Hopeless Cases…'

The statue of St Jude in the shrine was given by a petitioner. During the Second World War, a man wrote to ask for prayers for his wife, who was distraught over the recent death of their son, whose ship had been sunk. On learning that there was no statue of St Jude at the shrine, he offered a 16th century Spanish one which he had seen for sale in an antique shop in London. He requested that a small plaque be put up asking for prayers for the soul of his son 'lost at sea'. Fr Lynch thought this was premature and asked him to wait a while. Ten weeks later the son was found alive, a prisoner of war on a captured German sea raider.

Many artists helped to create this beautiful and peaceful shrine which, having been founded by the Carmelites, also had stained-glass windows and statues of the many Carmelite saints.

The level of devotion to St Jude in Faversham grew to such an extent that it nearly destroyed the shrine altogether. So many people wanted St Jude's help and lit so many candles as a sign of their prayer that in 2004, votive candles set the whole building alight. The shrine was badly damaged and for a while it seemed that the parish church would be lost also. In fact had the parish priest not been woken by the fire alarm, this

might have been the outcome. Amazingly the statue of
Saint Jude and reliquary survived although the windows,
mosaics and other works were destroyed. St Jude being
as he is however, the shrine was rebuilt with all the art
work as it had been before the fire, and was able to
celebrate its golden jubilee on 28th October 2005.

WRITINGS

The Letter of Saint Jude

Jude, a servant of Jesus Christ and brother of James, to those who are called, beloved in God the Father and kept for Jesus Christ: may mercy, peace and love be multiplied to you.

Beloved, being very eager to write to you of our common salvation, I found it necessary to write appealing to you to contend for the faith which was once for all delivered to the saints. For admission has been secretly gained by some who long ago were designated for this condemnation, ungodly persons who pervert the grace of our God into licentiousness and deny our only Master and Lord, Jesus Christ.

Now, I desire to remind you, though you were once for all fully informed, that he who saved a people out of the land of Egypt, afterward destroyed those who did not believe. And the angels that did not keep their own position but left their proper dwelling have been kept by him in eternal chains in the nether gloom until the judgment of the great day; just as Sodom and Gomorrah and the surrounding cities, which likewise acted immorally and indulged in unnatural lust, served as an example by undergoing a punishment of eternal fire.

Yet in like manner these men in their dreamings defile the flesh, reject authority, and revile the glorious ones. But when the archangel Michael, contending with the devil, disputed about the body of Moses, he did not presume to pronounce a reviling judgment on him, but said, 'The Lord rebuke you.' But these men revile whatever they do not understand, and by those things that they know by instinct as irrational animals do, they are destroyed. Woe to them! For they walk in the way of Cain, and abandon themselves for the sake of gain to Balaam's error, and perish in Korah's rebellion. These are blemishes on your love feasts, as they boldly carouse together, looking after themselves; waterless clouds, carried along by winds; fruitless trees in late autumn, twice dead, uprooted; wild waves of the sea, casting up the foam of their own shame; wandering stars for whom the nether gloom of darkness has been reserved for ever.

It was of these also that Enoch in the seventh generation from Adam prophesied, saying, 'Behold, the Lord came with his holy myriads, to execute judgment on all, and to convict all the ungodly of all their deeds of ungodliness which they have committed in such an ungodly way, and of all the harsh things which ungodly sinners have spoken against him.' These are grumblers, malcontents, following their own passions, loud-mouthed boasters, flattering people to gain advantage.

But you must remember, beloved, the predictions of the apostles of our Lord Jesus Christ; they said to you, 'In the last time there will be scoffers, following their own ungodly passions.' It is these who set up divisions, worldly people, devoid of the Spirit.

But you, beloved, build yourselves up on your most holy faith; pray in the Holy Spirit; keep yourselves in the love of God; wait for the mercy of our Lord Jesus Christ unto eternal life.

And convince some, who doubt; save some, by snatching them out of the fire; on some have mercy with fear, hating even the garment spotted by the flesh.

Now to him who is able to keep you from falling and to present you without blemish before the presence of his glory with rejoicing, to the only God, our Saviour through Jesus Christ our Lord, be glory, majesty, dominion and authority, before all time and now and for ever. Amen.

INTERCESSION TO ST JUDE

Prayer to St Jude

Glorious Apostle, Saint Jude Thaddeus, I praise God for all the graces he has bestowed upon you, granting you the privilege of bringing help to those in despair. Intercede for me in my great need. Through your merits and prayers may I receive the consolation of divine help in my necessity so that I may praise the mercy of God on earth and bless him eternally with you and all the elect in heaven. Ever mindful of your favour I will honour you as my heavenly patron, and encourage devotion to you in what way I can. Therefore with confidence I invoke your aid: helper when hope is fading, help me in my distress. Amen.

Prayer for St Jude's intercession

Lord, I praise and bless you and give you thanks for all graces and privileges you have bestowed upon your apostle, Saint Jude.

(Make your request here)

Lord, God, who revealed to St Jude your desire to be with us and share your life with us, open our hearts so that the Spirit may show us the truth and that keeping your commandments we may come to know your abiding presence.

We make this prayer through Christ Our Lord.

Our Father...

Hail Mary...

Glory Be...

Prayers for Various Needs

Prayer for help in time of need

(Can be used as a novena - once a day for nine days)

Saint Jude, faithful disciple and friend of Jesus, many have forgotten you because of the name of the man who betrayed the Master. But the church honours you, most holy Apostle, and invokes you as the universal patron of hopeless cases - of things despaired of. I ask you to intercede for me now in my time of need. Please bring help where help is almost despaired of, that I may receive consolation from the Lord in my suffering and assistance in my distress, particularly *[make your request]*. Trusting in the Lord's promise that whatever is asked in Jesus's name will be granted, I praise God for the many blessings I have already received from his generous love and look to the day when I can glorify him with all the saints in heaven. Amen. *(See also p30)*

Prayer in marital difficulties

Saint Jude, we are having problems with our marriage. Please, beg God to give us the light to see ourselves and each other as He sees us. Help us to grow in self-knowledge and mutual love. Help us to see and root out childish self-seeking and selfishness; to learn to love and be loved and to commit to each other every day of our marriage. Amen.

Prayer for a drug addict

Saint Jude, drug addiction has caused terrible suffering in my family. Help *(name)* to give up the drugs which are destroying his/her life. Help us his/her family to continue to love him/her. Amen.

Prayer of an alcoholic

Saint Jude, I beg your help in this sickness. Strengthen my weak faith. No matter what happens to me, teach me to be patient in troubles. Saint Jude, help me so that nothing weakens my determination to stay sober and abstain from alcoholic drink. Amen.

Prayer in mental illness

Compassionate Saint Jude, you have restored soundness of mind to so many through the power of God. See me *(or the person you are praying for)* in this suffering.

Confident of your powerful intercession, I beg you to ask Jesus, the merciful Healer, to restore me *(or the person you are praying for)* if it is God's will, that I *(he/she)* may experience once more the great gift of mental health. Amen.

Prayer in physical illness

Dear Saint Jude, I do not have the strength to pray as I should. My courage is faltering and loneliness and impatience cloud my mind and heart. Please obtain for me the courage and resignation I need to accept this trial from the hand of God with faith. If it is for the good of my soul, grant that I may recover my former health. Amen.

Prayer for the critically ill

Dear Apostle and Martyr for Christ, you left us an Epistle in the New Testament. With good reason many invoke you when illness is at a desperate stage. We now recommend to your kindness *[name]*, who is in a critical condition. If it is God's will, may the cure of this patient increase his/her faith and love for the Lord of Life, for the glory of our merciful God. Amen.

Prayer for spiritual help

Glorious Apostle and Martyr and Servant of Jesus, Saint Jude Thaddeus, you spread the true faith among barbarous and distant nations, and won to the obedience of Christ many peoples by the power of His Holy Word. Grant, I beg you, that from this day I may renounce every sinful habit, that I may be preserved from all evil thoughts, that I may always obtain your assistance, particularly in danger and difficulty, and that I may reach heaven with you to adore the Most Holy Trinity, the Father, Son and Holy Spirit, for ever. Amen.

Prayer in grievous affliction

Saint Jude, relative of Jesus and Mary, glorious Apostle and Martyr, renowned for your virtues and miracles, faithful and prompt intercessor for all who honour and trust in you, powerful patron and helper in grievous affliction, come to my aid, for you have received from God the privilege of helping those who almost despair. Look down on me; my cross is very heavy. My soul is enveloped in darkness and discouragement. Divine Providence is lost to my sight, and faith falters in my heart. Do not forsake me in this sad plight. I will not depart until you have heard me. Dear Saint Jude, hasten to my aid. Amen.

Prayer in financial worry

Dear Saint Jude, help me in this financial worry. I am not asking for wealth, but only for that immediate assistance which will enable me to meet my pressing obligations. I plead with you, help me to obtain the financial assistance I need in my present difficulty and teach me to see and use money as God would wish. Amen.

Prayer of praise and thanksgiving

Lord Jesus Christ, I praise, glorify and bless you for all the graces and privileges you have bestowed upon your chosen Apostle and intimate friend, Jude Thaddeus. I implore you, for the sake of his merits, grant me your grace and through his intercession come to my aid in all my need. Especially at the hour of my death, strengthen me against the power of the enemy. Amen.

Prayer on the death of a loved one

Saint Jude, you know how lonely I am since God took *(name)* to his/her eternal reward. Help me to see that taking *(name)* from me was not for my harm, but that I may look for him/ her always in God's presence. Amen.

Megalynarion

(a hymn from the Eastern Rite)

Come, let us acclaim the Apostle Jude, as the Master's kinsman and the initiate of His truth; for he sowed the glad tidings in tears and labours, but reaped a godly harvest in joy and blessedness.

LITANY

Litany in honour of St Jude

- for private use -

Lord, have mercy.

Christ, have mercy.

Lord, have mercy.

Christ, hear us.

Christ, graciously hear us.

God the Father of heaven, *have mercy on us*.

God the Redeemer of the world, *have mercy on us*.

God the Holy Spirit, *have mercy on us*.

Holy Trinity, one God, *have mercy on us*.

Saint Jude, relative of Jesus and Mary, *pray for us*.

Saint Jude, while on earth deemed worthy to see Jesus and Mary and enjoy their company, *pray for us*.

Saint Jude, raised to the dignity of an Apostle, *pray for us*.

Saint Jude, honoured in seeing the Divine Master humble himself to wash your feet, *pray for us*.

Saint Jude, who at the Last Supper received the Holy Eucharist from the hands of Jesus, *pray for us.*

Saint Jude, who after the profound grief which the death of your beloved Master caused you, had the consolation of seeing him risen from the dead and of assisting at his glorious Ascension, *pray for us.*

Saint Jude, filled with the Holy Spirit on the day of Pentecost, *pray for us.*

Saint Jude, who preached the Gospel in Persia, *pray for us.*

Saint Jude, who converted many people to the faith, *pray for us.*

Saint Jude, who performed wonderful miracles in the power of the Holy Spirit, *pray for us.*

Saint Jude, who restored an idolatrous king to health of both soul and body, *pray for us.*

Saint Jude, who imposed silence on demons and confounded their oracles, *pray for us.*

Saint Jude, who foretold to a weak prince an honourable peace with his powerful enemy, *pray for us.*

Saint Jude, who gloriously suffered martyrdom for the love of your Divine Master, *pray for us.*

Blessed Apostle, *with confidence we invoke you! (3 times)*

Saint Jude, help of the hopeless, *help me in my distress! (3 times)*

That by your intercession, both priests and lay members of the church may obtain an ardent zeal for the Faith of Jesus Christ, *hear us, we pray you.*

That you would defend our Sovereign Pontiff and obtain peace and unity for the church, *hear us, we pray you.*

That all unbelievers may receive the good news and be led to the Faith, *hear us, we pray you.*

That faith, hope and charity may increase in our hearts, *hear us, we pray you.*

That we may be delivered from evil thoughts and from the snares of the devil, *hear us, we pray you.*

That you would aid and protect all those who honour you, *hear us, we pray you.*

That you would preserve us from sin and all occasion of sin, *hear us, we pray you.*

That you would defend us at the hour of death against the fury of the devil and all evil spirits, *hear us, we pray you.*

Pray for us that before death we may expiate all our sins by sincere repentance and the worthy reception of the holy sacraments.

Pray for us that we may appease the divine justice and obtain a favourable judgment.

Pray for us that we may be admitted into the company of the blessed to rejoice in the presence of our God for ever.

Lamb of God, you take away the sins of the world, *spare us, O Lord.*

Lamb of God, you take away the sins of the world, *graciously hear us, O Lord.*

Lamb of God, you take away the sins of the world, *have mercy on us.*

Saint Jude, pray for us and for all who invoke your aid.

NOVENAS

What is a Novena?

A novena is nine days of prayer. When Jesus ascended into heaven he told the disciples to wait in Jerusalem and pray. After nine days of prayer the Holy Spirit descended on them at Pentecost. The nine days of prayer of a novena is in remembrance of those first nine days but the number itself is not magical and we can pray for our special intention for as many days as we need to.

Novena to Saint Jude

Day 1

O Blessed Apostle, Saint Jude, who laboured among the people of many lands and performed miracles in needy and despairing cases, I ask you to take interest in my need. You understand me. Hear my prayer and petition and plead for me. May I be patient in learning God's will for me and courageous in carrying it out.

Our Father…
Hail Mary…

Day 2

O Blessed Apostle, Saint Jude, grant that I may always serve the Lord as he deserves to be served, giving my best efforts and living as He wants me to live. May I use my heart and mind so that God will be disposed to listen to my petition, especially the one I entrust to you *[name it]*, and ask you to plead for me. May I be enlightened as to what is best for me and not forget the blessings I have received in the past.

Our Father...
Hail Mary...

Day 3

O Holy Saint Jude, who have so faithfully helped to spread the Gospel, I ask you to remember me and my needs. I specially pray for *[name it]*. May the Lord listen to your supplications on my behalf. May I always pray with fervour and devotion, resigning myself humbly to the Divine Will, seeing God's purpose in all my trials and knowing He will leave no sincere prayer unanswered in some way.

Our Father...
Hail Mary...

Day 4

Saint Jude, you were called to be one of Christ's chosen Apostles; listen with compassion to me, who ask your intercession. Plead for me that my petitions be answered especially *[name it]*. May God answer my prayer as He knows best, giving me grace to see His purpose in all things.

Our Father...
Hail Mary...

Day 5

O Holy Saint Jude, Apostle and companion of Jesus Christ, who lived a live of zeal, I entreat you to hear my prayers and obtain for me the following request *[name it]*. May I never forget the favours granted in the past and may I resign myself to God's holy will.

Our Father...
Hail Mary...

Day 6

Saint Jude, Apostle of Christ and helper in desperate cases, hear my prayer and petition. May I only seek what is pleasing to God and best for my salvation. Obtain this request for me *[name it]* if it be for the good of my soul. May I be resigned to God's will, knowing He will leave no request unanswered though it may be in an unexpected way.

Our Father...
Hail Mary...

Day 7

O Holy Apostle, Saint Jude, because Christ chose you as one of the Twelve, and because of your martyrdom, I know you are a close friend of God's. Therefore I do not hesitate to petition you for *[name it]*. I humbly submit to God's will in this. May I see His good purpose in all things.

    Our Father…
    Hail Mary…

Day 8

O Holy Saint Jude, pray that I may always imitate Christ and live in accordance with His will. I ask you to plead for me and obtain whatever is necessary for my salvation. I especially ask you to remember my request *[name it]*. May I co-operate with God's grace and accept the answer which He gives.

    Our Father…
    Hail Mary…

Day 9

O Holy Saint Jude, Apostle and Martyr, grant that I may live so as to be pleasing to God. Today I turn to you, asking you to intercede for me and obtain the favour I ask of God *[name it]*. But may I not seek temporal good only but rather what is good for my soul, seeing God's love for me in all my trials.

    Our Father…
    Hail Mary…

Novena to Saint Jude - to grow in Faith

Day 1

Saint Jude, you saw the healing power of Our Lord. You saw his compassion for the sick and dying. You yourself received authority to work miracles, to heal the sick and make people whole. We ask you to intercede with the Lord to send his saving grace on the sick and suffering, to comfort and encourage them. Amen.

Commitment
Today I commit to visiting someone who is sick or housebound.

Read: Lk 18: 35-43 and *Mk* 5: 25-34.

Day 2

Saint Jude, you asked God for the strength to evangelise. You trusted in God's mercy and love, knowing that nothing is impossible to Him. I ask you to pray for me now so that I may have the courage to place myself in God's loving hands. Amen.

Commitment
Today I commit to praying daily that God's will be done in me.

Read: Mt 14: 22-33 and *Lk* 11: 9-13.

Day 3

Saint Jude, you gave your life for others. You endured pain and martyrdom, gladly joining your sufferings to those of Our Saviour. I ask you to intercede for me so that I can remain faithful in the face of suffering. Help me to trust in God's love. Amen.

Commitment

Today I commit to offering up my sufferings no matter how large or small for the redemption of the world.

Read: Mt 27: 46 and *Col* 1: 24.

Day 4

Saint Jude, you courageously preached the word in all circumstances and when threatened with death you did not return violence for violence. Ask the Lord to give me courage to stand up for what is right and the faith to respond to injustice with love. Amen.

Commitment

Today I commit to praying to become a peacemaker.

Read: Mt 5: 9-12 and *Jn* 14: 27.

Day 5

Saint Jude, although you were chosen as one of the twelve, you learned not to be proud but to be humble and

serve. Intercede for me with Christ who humbled himself
on the cross to give me a spirit of service. Amen.

Commitment
Today I commit to doing some service for another.

Read: Mt 20: 26-28 and *Jn* 13: 34-35.

Day 6
Saint Jude, you learned to be merciful from the Son of
God who taught you to forgive those who persecuted
you and put you to death. Intercede for me today that
God will soften my heart to forgive others as He has
forgiven me. Amen.

Commitment
Today I will pray for someone who has offended me and
try to be reconciled with him/her.

Read: Mt 5: 44-48 and *Mt* 6: 7-15.

Day 7
Saint Jude, you opened yourself to God's will although
you knew you were not worthy to be His servant. Pray
for me today so that I can see that although I am very
weak with God all things are possible. Amen.

Commitment

Today I will offer myself to the Lord to be used in His service as He wishes.

Read: *Jn* 15: 15-16 and *Mt* 5: 13-16.

Day 8

Saint Jude, you are close to the Lord and know Him well. Intercede today for me that I might come to know Him intimately and feel the warmth of His loving presence in my life. Amen.

Commitment

Today I commit to making prayer the centre of my life.

Read: *Jn* 14: 23 and *Lk* 1: 46-55.

Day 9

Saint Jude, you gathered people together into communities of faith so that they could live the Gospel. You recognised the dignity of difference in all people and the equality of all in the sight of God. Help me not to judge as men do but as God does. Amen.

Commitment

Today I commit myself to offering services to my parish.

Read: *Gal* 3: 23-29 and *Ac* 2: 44-46.

Prayer of confidence

Let us pray O Lord, merciful Saviour, humbly I beseech you that having honoured the eternal memory of Saint Jude your kinsman and Apostle I may through his merits and prayers obtain the graces of your healing peace who live and reign world without end. Amen.

From the Feast of St Jude

Lord God, you taught us to call upon your name through the preaching of the apostles. At the intercession of Saint Jude may your church continue to grow by an increase in the number of believing nations. We make our prayer through Our Lord, Jesus Christ. Amen.

ACTS OF THE HOLY APOSTLE THADDAEUS, ONE OF THE TWELVE

Labbaeus who is also Thaddeus...came to Jerusalem to worship in the days of John the Baptist: and having heard his preaching and seen his angelic life, he was baptised...and having seen the appearing of Christ and His teaching and His wonderful works, he followed Him and became His disciple; and He chose him as one of the Twelve, the tenth apostle...

In those times there was a ruler of the city of Edessa, Agbar by name and there having gone abroad the fame of Christ, of the wonders He did and His teaching. Agbar, having heard of it, was astonished and desired to see Christ but could not leave his city and government. About the days of the Passion, Agbar was seized by an incurable disease and sent a letter to Christ by Ananias, the courier, to the following effect:

Agbar, Ruler of the city of Edessa, to Jesus the Saviour, the good physician, who has appeared in Jerusalem, Greetings -

I have heard about you and about the cures you perform without medicine or herbs. What I have heard is that you make the blind see again and the lame walk, you cleanse lepers, expel unclean spirits and demons, cure those who have suffered from chronic and painful diseases, and raise the dead. On hearing all this about you, I concluded that one of two things must be true - either you are God and came down from heaven to do these things, or you are God's son doing them. I am therefore writing to ask you to come to me and cure the illness from which I suffer. I have heard that the Jews are treating you badly and wish to cause you harm - my city is very small, but very noble, adequate for both of us to live in peace.

Agbar enjoined Ananias to take accurate account of Christ, of what appearance He was and His stature and His hair and everything about Him.

And Ananias, having gone and given the letter, was carefully looking at Christ, but was unable to fix Him in his mind. And Christ knew and asked to wash Himself and a towel was given to Him and when He had washed Himself, He wiped His face with it and His image having been imprinted on the linen, He gave it to Ananias saying 'Give this to him who sent you and tell him that after I have been taken up to heaven I will send my disciple Thaddeus to enlighten you and your city'... And having received the towel Agbar was cured of his disease.

After the Passion and the Resurrection and the Ascension, Thaddeus went to Agbar...and baptised him with all his house. And having instructed great multitudes of Hebrews and Greeks, Syrians and Armenians, he baptised them in the name of the Father and of the Son and of the Holy Spirit, and communicated to them the mysteries of the sacred body and blood of the Lord Jesus Christ... And Thaddeus...ordained as bishop one of his disciples, and gave them presbyters and deacons and the rule of the psalmody and the holy liturgy. And having left them he went to the city of Amis, the great metropolis of Syria-Mesopotamia, near the river Tigris. He went to the Synagogue on the Sabbath with his disciples and the High Priest asked where they came from and why they were there. And Thaddeus said, 'No doubt you have heard of what has taken place in Jerusalem about Jesus Christ. We are his disciples and witnesses of the wonderful things He did and taught. The chief priests delivered Him to Pilate out of hate and Pilate, being afraid, washed his hands in the sight of the multitude and gave Him to them. They took Him and spat on Him and mocked Him and crucified Him and laid Him in a tomb and secured it setting guards on it. On the third day He rose before dawn leaving His burial clothes in the tomb. He was seen first by his mother and by other women and then by Peter and John, my fellow disciples and then by all of us twelve. We ate and drank with Him after His Resurrection for many days. He sent us in His name to all the nations, to proclaim repentance and remission of sin and that those who were baptised would rise up incorrupt at the end of the age. He gave us power to expel demons and heal every disease and raise the dead.'

And the multitude, hearing this, brought their sick and Thaddeus laid his hand on them and healed them by calling on the name of Christ. And demoniacs were also healed, the spirits going out of them. And for many days the people ran from many places and hearing his teaching many believed and were baptised, confessing their sins.

Going round Syria he brought many cities to Christ, teaching and healing the sick and evangelising with his disciples.

(An apocryphal work - slightly different from
The Golden Legend.)

Directions to the Shrine of St Jude
in Tanners Street, Faversham

Arriving By Train

There is a railway station in Faversham itself. From London trains run from Victoria Station.

From Faversham Station turn right into Preston Street then left into Stone Street. At the end of Stone Street, turn right into South Street and then left into Tanners Street where you will see the church of Our Lady of Mount Carmel.

To get to the Shrine enter the church through the sacristy door. The door to the shrine is at the back of the church next to the statue of Our Lady of Mount Carmel.

Arriving by Car

Take the M2 and leave at Junction 6. Take the A251 and follow the signs for Faversham. When you get to a T junction with the A2, turn left and continue into Ospringe. Turn right at the Ship Inn, then take the 3rd left into Napleton Street. Turn left at the Three Tuns into Tanners Street. Pass the church, Our Lady of Mount Carmel, which will be on your right then turn right into the gate and follow the road round to the car park at the rear. There are steps up to the street.

To get to the Shrine enter the church through the sacristy door. The door to the shrine is at the back of the church next to the statue of Our Lady of Mount Carmel.

Compendium of the

CATECHISM OF THE
CATHOLIC CHURCH

"The *Compendium*, which I now present to the
Universal Church, is a faithful and sure synthesis of
the *Catechism of the Catholic Church*. It contains, in
concise form, all the essential and fundamental
elements of the Church's faith, thus constituting, as
my Predecessor had wished, a kind of *vademecum*,
which allows believers and non-believers alike to
behold the entire panorama of the Catholic faith.".

Benedictus PP XVI

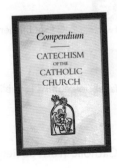

ISBN 978 1 86082 376 3

CTS Code: Do742

A world of Catholic reading at your fingertips...

Catholic Faith, Life & Truth for all

www.CTSbooks.org

twitter: @CTSpublishers

facebook.com/CTSpublishers

Catholic Truth Society, Publishers to the Holy See.